GROWING UP IN AFRICA

A DESTINY FULFILLED - A TRUE STORY OF COURAGE, OPTIMISM AND DETERMINATION IN THE FACE OF ADVERSITIES

DR. BENJAMIN OGBONNA

Kravitz & Sons

INNOVATORS IN PUBLISHING MARKETING AND ADVERTISING

Kravitz and Sons LLC
204 E Arlington Blvd. Suite B
Greenville, NC 27858

Published by Kravitz and Sons LLC.

ISBN: 979-8-89639-578-2 (sc)
ISBN: 979-8-89639-579-9 (e)

To the loving memory of my father Israel and my mother Grace.

Isn't it amazing how before the advent of the internet and other paraphernalia of modern life in Africa, children were able to meander through the maze of adversity and emerge to compete favourably with their more privileged counterparts from the western world? With no basic amenities such as electricity, running water, good healthcare, transportation, and all, you are encouraged to persevere, hoping for a brighter and more tolerable future by the grace of God.

Education in the face of all these shortcomings is a sine qua non. Without this, you are doomed to a life of permanent hardship till death. The society views as a failure the pursuit of any activity one is talented in except if it is geared towards the achievement of academic excellence.

This is a reflection of the life history of an African—a Nigerian to be specific. I chose Africa for a purpose. To every uninformed westerner, every black man is from Africa. For this category of people, Africa is an undeveloped country inhabited by starving and extremely poor people. The level of ignorance by seemingly educated people is astonishing. You get used to answering questions such as "How did you find your way to the United States or Britain?" for example. Did you come by bike or canoe?

Another interesting question I was confronted with on one occasion was "I gather the president is on his way to Africa. Will his plane be able to land?" I remember answering that the usual practice was for the president to land with a parachute, probably on top of a tree, and thereafter make his way to Mother Earth. Such was the level of ignorance some years ago, but the advent of the internet, I suppose, has helped to inform people about global affairs.

I am a physician by training, and I remember how, on several occasions, I have been informed by colleagues and other members of staff how they had a doctor from Africa a while ago called mutalungo or whatever, and you are asked whether you know him. You are supposed to, since he is black and from Africa. The doctor could well be from Zimbabwe, and you are from Nigeria. All blacks look alike and quite a significant number of westerners cannot differentiate them.

To be honest, the same applies to blacks coming to Europe for the first time. I had this problem when I first arrived in Britain for my postgraduate training. For the first time in my life, I saw a large concentration of white faces all around me, and I could barely differentiate one from the other.

As a dashing young doctor with the full complement of testosterone in my circulation, I was determined to get me a white girlfriend after a few months stay in Britain. Unbeknown to me, I found myself making overtures to two nurses at a time, thinking that I was dealing with the same nurse. They got to know my dilemma and decided to play along.

It was after I had adequately made a fool of myself over a long period of time that I got to realize my mistake. I was not let off easily. "Not so fast, lover boy," I was told. They decided to confront me to rub it in. I apologized profusely and confessed it was not a deliberate action as I was not aware I was dealing with two individuals. They were sympathetic though. One of them said, "We will let you off, but you must make tea for all of us during break time."

During break, I proceeded to make tea for everybody. The only problem was that at that time, being new in the United Kingdom, I was not aware that there was a protocol to it. After brewing the tea, I proceeded to pour the tea into the tea cups, and just as I was about to pour milk into the tea, a nurse walked in and said, "What are you doing? Is that the way you make tea?" Apparently, you pour tea into milk and not the other way around. You may consider this as not a big deal, but it is, especially in a society where drinking of tea is cherished as national way of life.

This nurse was impressed however that I was making tea for everybody. "Doctors are not known to be generous and are mostly selfish towards other members of staff," she acknowledged. If only she knew I was being punished for being naughty, she wouldn't have had such a high impression about me.

Despite making the tea, I ended up losing both nurses, but we remained good friends. They now and again draw my attention to the embarrassing situation just for a good laugh. I tried to put this behind me and get on with my life as if nothing happened, to no avail.

Just as all blacks look alike to a white person, whites look very much alike when one arrives from Africa for the first time. You learn the hard way, don't you?

This story cannot be remotely referred to as my autobiography. It cannot be, because I am not a celebrity. Autobiography is for the rich and famous. These are people who have it all, and they get to write about their life history which we all fall over each other to buy, and if you are lucky, you get your copy autographed.

On the other hand, you can refer to this write-up as the autobiography of a not-so-famous doctor, originally from a remote village in Nigeria—a doctor who, against all the odds, including a civil war, made it to Europe, United States, and the Middle East. The sky, they say, is the limit for those that aim high. Quoting late Professor Hawking, "You look up to the stars and not down at your feet."

There are people in the western world who wonder how these professionals coming from Africa go about getting themselves educated as to be able to compete with their counterparts in the western world. Mind you, the story today is not the same as several years ago because of the advent of computers and the world becoming a global village. People are a lot better informed today than they were in the '50s and '60s. Those were the days you were asked whether you had come over to study English despite speaking perfect Queen's English, albeit with an accent. As long as you have an accent, no matter how you try, people are bound to make you repeat yourself. You make a fool of yourself if you try to fake the foreign accent you find yourself in.

As a result, over the years, I have maintained an accent that is peculiar to me. People ask me whether I am from the Caribbean or some other place but not Nigeria.

No matter how simple and easy your name is, you are made to spell it, as long as it is not a biblical or Western European name. Eastern European names are easy to pronounce, including those that do not contain vowels. I have a complicated middle name which I was going to substitute for my surname to make it even more difficult but was compelled to abandon the idea by my father.

As I stated earlier, call it my autobiography or not, this is an account of my life history, starting from birth to my semi-retirement as an obstetrician and gynecologist. Wouldn't it be nice to read about someone who cannot, by any stretch of the imagination, be regarded as a celebrity worthy to write about? Doctors are never known to be celebrities no matter what they do. Our calling demands that you go about your job without fanfare.

I have on several occasions wished that we do get a bit of our reward here on earth rather than wait to go to heaven before you are compensated.

Having said this, I consider my job very satisfying and endearing indeed. Take for example, the birth of a newborn male child. The family turns around to ask, "What's your name, doctor?" and promptly the baby is named after you. Come to think of it, there are so many babies out there named after me, and nothing can be more rewarding. It is obvious therefore that we do indeed get our reward here on earth after all, without realizing it.

In discussing my life history, I will discuss my birth and my escapades growing up. I will also discuss how I survived the civil war, my education, travels, and other bits and pieces so long as my recollection does not fail me.

As I was reflecting on my life, it suddenly dawned on me there was a recurrent pattern to my milestone, dating back to my childhood. It became obvious that there was a constant cyclical nature, since there was a transition that occurred every ten years in my life and the decade always begins and ends with the year ending with the number six (e.g. 2006–2016).

With this in mind, I was able to categorize my life history into ten yearly intervals starting from my preteen years well into adulthood. I will summarize the pattern and lay out the transition for every decade, compartmentalizing the events that marked the period.

First Phase (Birth–1956): Kindergarten through elementary school

Second Phase (1956–1966): Completion of elementary school, high school, and beginning of the Nigerian civil war

Third Phase (1966–1976): Survival of civil war, through to completion of medical school

Fourth Phase (1976–1986): Travel to United Kingdom for postgraduate specialization

Fifth Phase (1986–1996): Departure from United Kingdom to Saudi Arabia working for ministry of health as specialist/consultant

Sixth Phase (1996–2006): Retirement from Saudi Arabian oil company after ten years of service

Seventh Phase (2006–2016): Retirement from the National Health Service NHS

Eighth Phase (2016 till date): Enjoying life as a senior citizen

First Phase (Birth–1956)

I was born in a small village in Eastern Nigeria to a middle-class, or I should say, lower-middle-class family. I was the second of seven children.

The story of my birth, as told by my mother, was that immediately after birth, at the time newborns are struggling to open their eyes to focus and acclimatize to the new environment, I came out staring at my mother. The stare was so intense that my mother was frightened according to her. "What manner of child will come out with such an intense stare as if angry at being delivered?" she always wondered. The significance of this event is anybody's guess.

My father was a headmaster, a position that was so much revered and respected in those days in the society. Therefore, I can lay claim to being born to a middle-class family. As a headmaster, my father achieved what would be extremely difficult to achieve these days. He was able to train not only his immediate children but also those of his brother, numbering eight. The most appropriate appellation for the family as composed is a clan.

Being the son of a headmaster in those days came with certain privileges which I took full advantage of. I was naughty and stubborn growing up. I remember disrupting the class as a four-year-old and to be reprimanded by the teacher to no avail. I was punished by a knock on the head to quieten me. I was not going to have it, and I retaliated by placing the teacher's stool beside him, climbed up it, and gave him a knock on his head for good measure in retaliation. What followed this incident is anybody's guess. I was disciplined by the teacher and my father.

Those were the days we start with a slate and chalk at preschool until you graduate to using paper and pencil. My mother used to have a nightmare dealing with my school uniform coated with a variety of assorted colours of chalk. There were days I would forget my slate at school with my long-suffering mother going over to retrieve it.

Don't even get me started with the next stage, which is the use of bottled ink and a nib, as the writing material was called. You dip the nib in the ink and commence writing. Dipping and writing is a continuous affair as the ink on the nib dries within seconds. A complete mess, you would reckon. Most often than not, the bottled ink spills over the notebook and the desk. You get punished no matter the cause of the spillage. As the ink is usually difficult to wash off, you move on with your school uniform coated with smudges of ink.

My care-free attitude to life dated back to the early part of my life.

I remember one occasion when I went out with my brothers to gather fruits. I left my shoes out there and walked back home without realizing that I had my shoes on when I left the house. It was late at night when I realized my shoes were missing. I had to because I had only one pair. I would have preferred my mother to take me to go find the shoes, but because it was late at night, my father took me. I got the beating of my life all the way from the house to where I left them.

Those were the days when it is said that the fear of a headmaster is the beginning of wisdom. Corporal punishment was the order of the day. You were not immune to discipline being the son of a headmaster. The beating did not deter me as I continued with my carefree approach to life with reckless abandon.

I remember on one occasion during English class when my father taught that using the expression "Don't be silly" was not considered an insult. After a period of fifteen to twenty minutes while the lesson was ongoing, a classmate tried to test his luck by telling my father, "Don't be silly." No doubt, he ended up with twelve strokes of the cane while mounted on the back of another classmate. From that day till date, I have not used that expression for anybody, certainly not an elderly person out of respect.

Suffice it to say that the shoes were exactly where I left them. Stealing was alien to our culture in those days. These days the shoes would have disappeared within a minute of my departure from the scene.

I was a bit wild growing up. I remember when as a five-year-old, I fell from a tree only to be rescued by my "jumper." The jumper got stuck to a branch, and I was flailing with nothing to hold on to until some Good Samaritan rescued me.

Being the son of a headmaster and a missionary meant traveling to very remote parts of Nigeria. Some of these places can be very hostile environment, and you get to meet and interact with all sorts of people and characters. Fighting was the order of the day. The unwritten rule in the house was that if you get beaten up by anybody your age, you will get a second beating by your father. If on the other hand, you are beaten by someone older than you, one of your senior brothers will be sent out to settle the score on your behalf.

Even my mother was not exempted from this rule. I remember one occasion when we were out playing. My younger brother unwittingly stepped on a pool of water which splashed on a young kid carried by his mother. The woman slapped my brother who was only six years old, not taking into considering that this was not deliberate. As per the rule of the house, I dashed back home to inform my mom that there was a job for her. She came right over and heaved the woman off her feet and tossed her into a ditch for daring to slap her son.

Despite these, we were trained to be respectful and to avoid getting into trouble as much as possible. Peradventure you find yourself at the wrong end of the stick, you are given the option to choose between your mom or dad who to discipline you.

To this day, I have a phobia for snakes. How did this come about? Living in remote and underdeveloped parts also entailed seeing all sorts of dangerous and not-so-dangerous animals and reptiles. For some inexplicable reason, I was seeing all manner of snakes every single day and at no time was I bitten by one.

I remember this particular incident when I arrived with my father to a teacher's house to pass the night before continuing our journey home as it was late and dangerous to continue. It was dark outside, and they had gone to bed. My father knocked on the door, and the houseboy came and opened the door to let us in. As soon as the door was opened, a snake appeared from nowhere and bit him. The poor chap who had gone to bed and came out to open the door was bitten by a snake that emerged from outside the house. That none of us standing out there waiting to be let in was not bitten by the snake lurking around the corner was a miracle. If this was not a miracle, I don't know what else is.

Glad to say that the boy had a first-aid from my father and was taken to the hospital where he made a full recovery. I am also glad to say that despite spending two years in this snake-infested environment, none of us were bitten.

The story about snakes will not be complete without mentioning my mother, who will fight and kill any snake no matter the size or shape. The same woman had a phobia for the millipede. This is a very small and harmless creature that goes about its business. When you see her running and screaming, you can safely assume she is running from a millipede. While I took care of the millipedes, my mother would deal with the snakes. This way, everybody's role was well defined. Thank you very much!

For water supply, we make do with walking a considerable distance to fetch from a pond or a river depending on where we were. I remember one occasion when my mother lost her footing trying to fetch water from a pond and started to drown in my presence. I was only six years old, and I stood there watching helplessly. She pulled herself out, clutching to what could pass as a shrub. She was glad I did not attempt to rescue her as that would have meant both of us drowning. This was another miracle that this time around happened to a woman of faith.

Getting up early in the morning to go to the stream in search of water is not an excuse to be late for school. Most of the times, the headmaster, who is your father, will be the one rounding up all the late comers. You are not spared the cane despite the fact he is aware of why you were late. This source of water for household chores must be responsible for my chronic health issues.

Malaria from mosquito bites was a major problem. Before going to bed, you will spend time killing the mosquitoes that got big feeding on you that they have problems getting out of the net. They find their way in but after feeding can no longer get out. The problem with malaria is not the fever but the side effect of the medication my father treats us with. It used to be quinacrine in those days. The itching that comes with it keeps you scratching for days on end. One episode of scratching comes to mind. This was so intense I was rolling round the floor and inadvertently stumbled across a five-pound note that fell off the pocket of a visitor. Since I was not going to declare the money to my parents, I pocketed it, and it had a soothing effect to my suffering.

In addition to malaria, I was noted for constant abdominal pain far more than the rest of my siblings. Though we were drinking and eating from the same source, I was reacting to whatever germ that was in the drinking water more than the rest.

Talking about abdominal pain leads to an incident I wish to recount. I was about seven years old when on this particular day I had abdominal pain all day long. My mother tried everything to help relieve the colic but was unsuccessful. Unfortunately, the nearest hospital was six miles away. Getting to the hospital meant trekking the distance or riding a bike. There were no other means of transportation. The journey to the hospital was fraught with all sorts of danger from wild animals and bandits. It was a very hostile environment and a journey to the hospital at night was fraught with all sorts of unimaginable dangers. For light, my father hung a lantern on the handlebar of the cycle. This was the dilemma my father was confronted with when my abdominal pain persisted.

It must have been around midnight when he read his Bible and got me on his bike to take me to the hospital. We were only about three minutes ride from the house when an elderly woman carrying a load on her head emerged from nowhere and blocked the way. My father unwittingly rammed the bike over this lady, and we all ended up in the bush. You may not believe this, but my pain stopped there and then. I told my father that the pain had gone, and he took me back home. Nothing happened to this lady, and to the best of my knowledge, to this day I was not sure where the lady was headed or where she came from. Nothing about this woman was ever mentioned or discussed by my father.

It would appear that this lady materialized to save us from the danger we would have encountered had the journey continued. Who was this woman? Could she be an angel sent from God? This no doubt was a mystery or miracle, if you like. I recall that after this incident, I never had abdominal pain ever again. You might be thinking that I was faking the abdominal pain. No, I wasn't, to be honest. The picture of angels in white flowing robes and large wings flying all over the place must be far from the truth. I believe that angels appear in human form and interact with us now and again to deliver their message.

Did I see an apparition of a fair-complexioned mother and her child up in the sky at the age of two or three? Yes, I did, and the picture has remained clear in my memory to this date. The mental recollection of what I saw and what I was doing at that tender age remains vividly clear in my memory. My mother, though she was standing out there with me, did not see the apparition, and being very young, I could not tell her what I was looking at. Over the years, I have only confided to close relatives about this vision. Why the apparition was that of a smiling lady with her child on her laps remains a mystery. With knowledge of hindsight, it does appear that this was a forerunner of what I was destined to be later in life. Whatever it was had to do with mother and child.

How would you explain the fact that throughout my preschool and kindergarten years, drawing the cross on my forehead with a chalk or a marker was more of a reflex action than something done deliberately? I come back home from school or playing with friends with the cross drawn on my forehead. This was a habit I had no answer to. I do recollect my mom wiping this off my forehead most times.

Was I then destined to be a man of God only to fall by the wayside to become a doctor? I do not know the answer to this question. I suppose that since I do not have the ability to make speeches and pull the crowd, I would have been a very poor pastor indeed. It would have been a case of when I am done with my sermon, there would be nobody left in the congregation. They would all be asleep or be dead with boredom. Some will even quietly sneak away. On the other hand, since God works in a mysterious way, I would probably have been a charismatic man of God if I chose that line. He has the power to loosen my tongue and infuse in me the power of the Holy Spirit. It would appear therefore that this was a destiny that was never fulfilled.

You get to have a new dress made for you at Christmas and sometimes Easter if you are lucky. What used to pass as a Christmas dress is a piece of clot stitched together by my mom and called jumper. It usually had two side pockets and nothing else. I remember we wore these with our school shorts or underpants with no shoes. I didn't take kindly to this and consequently was always falling foul of my parents and getting a good reprimand. In no way was I going to church where I am likely to see a classmate, probably a girl, with no shoes on. What I did in those days was to wander off with friends looking for wild fruits while the service lasted. When the service was over, and we got back home, my father or my mother would ask where I was as he or she could not recall seeing me at all. This unfortunately was a recurrent event as I was determined not to be seen in my Christmas dress without a pair of shoes.

This is my recollection of my preteen years. Despite all these adversities, education continued unabated, and I was able to go through my elementary school education without problems. Education I must say was thorough in those days. As an African child, there was no alternative.

At the age of eight to nine, I was bold enough and able to read Bible portions to the entire school now and again during morning devotions. This was the age I joined the choir but left after a few months due to unforeseen circumstances.

What happened was that the choir was supposed to render a song which we spent time preparing. The music teacher was so elated at his success that he looked forward to the event with pride. This was supposed to be a big service with the bishop in attendance. We got up to render our song, and as usual he used his "tuning fork" to get us started. There was no piano or organ available. Try as much as he did, we could not get the tune right. After three attempts, with the choir singing off tune, we were requested to take our seats. What happened next was that after service, the choirmaster was so infuriated that he gave each of us twelve strokes of the cane. You could imagine me going home after service with a sore back. I did not mention this to my mom or dad or the choirmaster would have faced the wrath of my parents.

After this incident, I left the choir, and to this day, I have never found myself anywhere near a choir. The result of this was that over the years I lost my voice so much so that I make sure nobody hears me singing during church services. Our singing off-tune was not as a result of my bad voice. My voice was crisp and clear in those days. I continue to blame the choirmaster for flogging me, I probably would have made a successful career as a musician. I now play the organ for personal or family pleasure instead.

There was one occasion when one gentleman sitting next to me in the church had a voice as bad as mine. We both struggled through a difficult hymn, at the end of which he leant over to tell me, "That was a tricky one."

"You can say that again" was my response. We were both singing with discordant tunes while making sure the person sitting next to you did not hear you struggling. Thanks to the choirmaster.

Before delving into my teenage years, a period that saw me through secondary school, or high school if you like, I must mention another event that can also pass as a miracle.

Towards the end of my primary school education, I passed the entrance examination to one of the few Anglican Mission High Schools for boys at that time and was invited for an interview. Getting to this school from where my father was stationed was quite a journey. As there were no taxis or buses, travelling had to be by lorry. The lorry then was a big truck with benches which made for a very uncomfortable ride. Added to this was an untarred road with potholes. With all these, you begin to fully appreciate the agony one went through, even for a short journey. Being a young kid with my feet dangling while seated on these benches, you maintain stability by sandwiching yourself between two passengers.

I liked the school because it was in a big city. My father dropped me off at the school and went back to the parish to see the pastor. He was a well-known missionary after all. After the interview, I found my father playing the church organ, which he was very good at. I knew he was an organist, but that was the first time I saw him play. He was noticeably excited, and he spent a considerable length of time playing at the church. When he was done playing, he wondered whether it would ever be possible for him to be posted to a place where he could have the opportunity to have an organ at his disposal to play. The church was only a mile from the high school.

Two weeks after the interview, I got a letter informing me that I was successful. In what could pass as a miracle, a couple of weeks after my letter, my father also received an unexpected news informing him that he had been promoted to the position of inspector of schools for the Anglican Communion and was posted to the very same parish where he stopped over when I went for my interview.

The pastor had nothing to do with this posting since the post was well above his sphere of influence and he had an organist for his church. His office was thirty-six miles away, and this location was judged to be central to enable him to cover the entire state. The pastor had to be approached to allow my father use of his guesthouse as a temporary accommodation. I am in no doubt that this was a clear case of divine intervention. This was how my parents and siblings came to live in a location one mile from my high school. They remained there throughout the five years I spent in high school.

Second Phase (1956–1966)

It was a boarding school, but with my parents around the corner, I developed the habit of sneaking out now and again for one reason or the other. The risk of being caught by the principal or school prefect made these trips very risky indeed. As a teenager, the tension and adrenalin were part of the fun. I remember the one occasion I sneaked out and was caught by the principal. I had a nice ride back to the school in his car but faced the music the next day. I was brought out after morning devotion, and after my offence was read out by the principal, I faced the inevitable punishment. This involved uprooting a palm tree. You are not expected to truly uproot the palm tree. You are usually let off after one or two days depending on the gravity of your offense. You don't belong to the elite group if you have not gone through this punishment. If you think I will be deterred after this punishment, you will be mistaken. I was not deterred, and I continued the trips, sometimes making a dash for the bush when I see a car that remotely resembled the principal's.

For some reason during my preteen years I was obsessed with being a doctor, and through high school, I made sure I took all the courses that would eventually lead to my achieving my ambition to become a doctor. I was good at the sciences and mathematics. I was not particularly good with the arts subjects. As a matter of fact, I dropped history when the teacher punished me for being disruptive in class. I was almost tempted to drop religion, but the fear of my father prevailed. He would have simply pulled me out of school.

The teachers were dedicated and well educated. Our syllabus and education system were modeled after the standard of any good British high school. Unbeknown to the students in the United Kingdom, students in Nigeria were being trained at the same level as they were, albeit with limited facilities. Whatever we lacked in infra-structure was made up by our determination to succeed at all cost. Whereas students in the western world can be complacent sometimes because everything is available for them, the reverse is the case for us. Nothing was easy as one had to work very hard.

At the high school, electricity was from a generator tucked away some meters from the school to avoid the sound nuisance that goes with it. Lights come on at 6:00p.m. and out at 10:00p.m. Switching the generator on and off was the responsibility of the students. A task that is taken in turns. I dreaded the idea of going late at night to turn off the generator and coming back to the dormitory with a touch light. Luckily, one of my classmates saw the dilemma I was in and graciously skipped me when it was my turn. I remained grateful to him ever after. Thereafter, there was no electricity the rest of the night and day.

The principal of the school was a white man from Kent in England. He was a pastor of the Anglican Communion as well as an educationist. Our training was modeled out of the British High School protocol.

Our daily routine was also similar. We grew up to be polished English students without stepping foot in England. The bell rings at six in the morning, and everybody hurries out for an hour of exercise. After the exercise, it is time for shower followed by breakfast. As soon as breakfast is over, we head straight to the chapel for morning devo-tion at the end of which announcements are made. Thereafter we head to the classrooms for the days lectures. After lecture, it is time for lunch before retiring for siesta. At the end of siesta, it is time for manual labour and spotting activities. When the bell rings, we retire for shower again and get ready for dinner. Dinner is followed by night preps during which homework and other academic activities are done. At 10:00p.m., the bell is rung for evening devotion after which we retire for lights out. Talk about discipline, this is it.

Nigeria is blessed with the best weather in the world. When it rains, it pours, and for a period of time everywhere remains cool. Air conditioning was for the rich. It is something you could comfortably do without. At night while it is raining, the sound from the zinc roof is soothing to the extent that you do not need any medication to send you to sleep. Insomnia is not a common complaint from people in that part of the world.

For water supply, we draw from the well. In my school, there was only one well serving the entire institution. Each dormitory is apportioned a time interval during which to draw from the well. If you miss your slot, you are done for the day. When the well dries up for one reason or the other, we wake up very early in the morning to go to the stream to fetch water to wash with and get ready for classes. It was during one of the trips to the stream that a group of senior students were having a bath unbeknown to them, that there were some girls from an adjoining school around. These girls took off with the shorts and pants of these students, and they came back to school wearing their towels for good measure. Later that night, the entire school took off to go retrieve the seized apparels only to be confronted by the school principal who addressed the issue. While the demonstration lasted, I took the opportunity to sneak home for some homecooked food.

My high school years were mostly uneventful. It was a five-year program after which I did two years for the higher school certificate and general certificate examination advanced level. It was very easy to secure a good job after high school in those days, but for someone aspiring for higher education, I was not tempted. Life generally was a lot better for the family. We were now living in a more civilized part of the world and rapidly adjusting to a new life. My father now had a car, and we were no longer travelling on trucks or bicycles as before.

I was still a teenager when I finished my advanced level education and was looking forward to entering the university for my lifelong ambition to train as a doctor. As expected, I took physics, chemistry, and zoology at advanced level to qualify for admission into medical school. There is usually a waiting period of nine months before entering the university. This is the period higher school certificate holders pick up teaching assignments in high schools to make some money which will come handy in due course. This was an interesting experience for me since this was my first job. I had money to spend far more than I ever had in my life. Away from the prying eyes of my very strict parents, I took to smoking and drinking—just being the teenager that I was. This was more a peer pressure thing as one had to "belong," The problem was that my father once again was living only two miles away from my school, and the principal of the school was his student several years back. I was promptly reported, and I was summoned to face the music. My punishment was that I was to surrender my entire salary at the end of each pay period and given only a pittance for subsistence. I was at liberty however to trek home when I wanted to eat. I survived and was looking forward to the end of my teaching career.

Towards the time the nine months was coming to an end, I started limbering up in preparation to becoming a medical student. You could actually see the swagger in my steps, and I noticed that I was getting more attention from the students. It was a mixed institution. It was at this time that I had my first girlfriend. The principal got to know that I had a girlfriend amongst the senior girls and was not amused. You can guess what he did. You are correct! He reported me to my father, and my father simply did not have a clue how to go about this particular problem. Strangely enough he just ignored me.

Third Phase (1966–1976)

 Just around the time I was about to leave, the unexpected happened. A tragedy would be the appropriate description of the event that was to unfold. A civil war that was to take a solid four years out of my educational progress commenced. My swagger turned expectedly to a limp as I prepared for a journey to the unknown.

The event of the civil war is a topic that will take another write up. For this essay however, I will recount salient events that occurred during the entire duration of the war.

I survived whatever it was that I went through as I am alive to be able to recount my life history. A dead man does not write autobiography. With the rapidly unfolding events and the fact that schools were no longer in session, I lost my swagger, and all my effort was now channeled towards survival. I was still a teenager when the war started.

You will recall that prior to the commencement of the civil war, I had always lived with my parents just around the corner. It was mostly a fight for survival away from the prying eyes of my parents.

I am aware a lot has been written about the Nigeria civil war or Biafran war as those of us in Biafra at the time called it. I will however mention salient aspects of the war that I was involved with.

This will include as usual mysterious or miraculous escapes that saw me survive the war. With all that I have recounted so far, you will agree with me that there is, without an iota of doubt, what can aptly be referred to as destiny. From my account thus far, there is no doubt that right from childhood there is that something, which I believe is God looking down on me, that helps me to overcome whatever adversity I am confronted with. I was destined to overcome all the odds, from my stuttering steps in life to adulthood in order to fulfill the assignment God kept for me.

My strict Christian upbringing meant that once your heart is free from any mischief, and your hands are clean, you only need to march on and leave the rest to God. I must confess, however, that my marching on was tinged occasionally with a bit of recklessness and naivety. With the war raging, one did not have the luxury of wavering in one's belief or faith. I remained a good Christian despite staying away from church during childhood just because of the jumper my mom used to sew for us if you recall.

For families during the war, it was a question of everyone to himself or herself and God for us all. I left my parents and was not to see them till the war was over after three years. You are so preoccupied with survival that you did not bother to know what was happening to your parents and siblings. The only source of information was the radio and telephone as we know it was nonexistent.

Hunger was the order of the day, and reaping where one did not sow was common practice. You brazenly and boldly walked into someone's farm and started harvesting to feed yourself. This was not considered stealing. All you do is apologize and move on. God in his infinite mercy knew we had no choice, and we were forgiven there and then.

At the early stage of the war, I had training in civil defense and worked as a guard on road blocks mounted at strategic portions of the highway. I fled after a couple of months when a military officer, delivering military equipment, blasted his driver for stopping to be checked rather than crushing us. That was the last straw even though there had not been a previous straw. I was having none of it, and I fled never to return to my beat.

Although my aim was to join the army as an officer, I was bidding my time. From the militia, I joined the police force but left after the training. Don't ask me why. I refused to show up for duty for whatever reason. Becoming a police officer just didn't click with me.

It was at this stage that my father showed an emotional reaction towards me that hitherto was alien to him. He realized my restlessness and "begged" me to avoid joining the army for the sake of the family. To my recollection, this was the only time I can recall my father showed some emotions. I am talking about a headmaster who throughout his life had laid down rules that must be obeyed.

His students that knew him insist that the fear of my father was the beginning of wisdom. Strangely enough, he was not bothered whether any of my other siblings joined the army. Being a man of God, he probably had a premonition that I probably would not survive the war if I joined the army. I reckon he saw me as his child who plunges in head first into danger before stopping to think.

Whatever the case, my father knew me a lot more than I knew myself. It is said that only parents know their children.

Throughout my childhood, I could not shoot and kill a bird with my catapult. Try as I could, I always come back empty handed. The situation was so bad that my siblings used to joke that when birds see me coming towards them with my catapult, they reassure themselves not to bother flying away as this one can do no harm to them. While my siblings make fun of me, my father will reassure me and encourage me to keep trying. My younger brother who later joined the military shoots to kill and never misses. When the birds sighted him from afar, they flew away and would not perch until he leaves the scene. "It is the bad one that is coming," they seem to say. This probably influenced my father to stop me joining the military at all cost.

Despite the warning from my father not to join, I ignored him and made three attempts without success.

The first time around, as a proud owner of the higher school certificate and the general certificate of education advanced level, which I displayed prominently during the selection parade for admission into the officer cadet school, I expected to be selected as I was more qualified than a good majority of the other candidates. At the parade ground during the interview, the recruiting major came to me, sized me up from head to toe, ordered me out of the line, and hollered at me to "get the hell out of here and go home and have a haircut." I was disappointed, and I did not mention what transpired to my father or he would have had a good laugh.

I made two more unsuccessful attempts with one thing or the other disqualifying me. I was determined however that on no account was I going to join the army as an ordinary recruit because of my qualification.

The war meanwhile continued to rage. As teenagers, all we did each morning was to assemble somewhere around the city to gossip and play games oblivious of the ferocious bombings that occurred.

By games, I don't mean video games as there was nothing like that around. You will be lucky to see a black-and-white television if your family is rich. This was the case until bombs began to rain from the sky all over the place. We were so naïve and fearless, thinking that bombs were not meant for us. I remember standing out there during an air raid with a friend, pointing at the plane that was flying very low across the city, not realizing that machine guns were being fired from the rear end of the plane in addition to bombs that were being dropped. I could have been shot.

It was during this period of roaming aimlessly in the city that a gentleman approached me and requested that I show him my palm to be read. I never knew the gentleman, and he looked weird. Surprisingly I obliged him. This man spent some time reading my palm, and while this lasted, I noticed he had a grin on his face. I wondered what the hell he was grinning at.

When he was done, he turned around and told me that he saw me traveling the whole world. He also told me about my finances as well as what my marital history was going to be. I wondered how someone, in the midst of a gruesome war, a war I was not sure I was going to survive, will travel extensively in future.

The situation I found myself at this point in time was a situation where if you did not die of hunger, you are likely to come to some harm through a bomb, gunshot, or any accident.

The three significant events about my life this strange man told me about my life as written on my palm were correct to the letter. I will not go into details over two of the predictions, but as you read on, you will appreciate that his prediction about travels was true.

Much as you guess about the other two, I will not disclose these. Suffice it to say that those other aspects of my life will be subject of another discussion in due course.

I will now discuss my first brush with death during the civil war. At this stage of the war, I was living with my elder brother in the city.

He was charged with the responsibility of keeping an eye over me and reporting back to my dad what mischief I was up to.

As I mentioned earlier, I had a group of friends, more like the boys and girls in town. All that we did each day was to assembly in a friend's house and while away our time. This was a daily routine and we all met each day and hopefully one of us would provide the food for us to eat. When one of us gets a "stick" of cigarette, it will be shared amongst those of us that smoke. It was simply a question of taking three or four puffs and passing it on to the next in line. There was no pocket money or any source of income. I had this habit of puffing away and finishing my share in one go without leaving any for later in the night. When my friend, who is wiser, gets his remaining bit later at night, I resort to begging him for just a puff. He always obliged me but continued to admonish me to learn to leave some for a rainy day without success. I will repeat the same thing next time and come begging as usual.

One day, my senior cousin who was a top military officer fighting in one of the war fronts dispatched his orderly and driver to come pick me up to spend some time with him. Although he was in active war theatre, he knew I was not going to be in danger, and all he wanted was my company and of course to have some good food to eat.

Without informing my elder brother, I quietly sneaked out of the house and travelled. I was away for two weeks, and when I came back, all hell was let loose. After a thorough dressing down from my elder brother, I was taken to my father who finished the rest. They rightly thought I had come to some harm or dead.

Undaunted, the next day after my arrival, I went back to meet my friends, and one of them pulled me aside to ask whether I was aware of what happened. I was dumbfounded when he told me that a day after I travelled, a bomb fell on the particular spot where we normally assembled, and a good number of my friends including my girlfriend were killed. It dawned on me there and then that once again I had cheated death as there was no doubt I would have been at that same spot on that fateful day. This, once again, was a case of divine intervention. My cousin was used by God to rescue me from what could have been the end.

My story will continue because I am still alive! Death was no longer a big deal considering the number of deaths one encountered each day. Within a week of my trip back, we found ourselves a new meeting place, and life continued.

When the city finally fell to the Nigerian forces, we fled to various directions. It was like a domino effect the rate at which the cities were falling to the advancing Nigerian forces. All we did was that when we sensed danger, we packed up and left to nowhere as long as it was a good distance from the sound of gunfire, shelling, and bombs. As there were no bikes, cars, or trucks for transportation, we could trek for miles, in some cases twenty miles, without breaking sweat. Where do you get the painkillers for sore feet? One is tempted to ask; the answer is nowhere. You make do by massaging your sore and swollen feet with hot water, and that was it.

Because the war was going against us, there was an active conscription of whoever was strong enough to carry a machine gun, the age notwithstanding. On my part, I was determined not to be conscripted having presented myself on three occasions to be enlisted, albeit against the advice of my parents. I was however conscripted on three occasions, and on each occasion a group of well-armed soldiers will materialize to get me out.

On one of the occasions after I was conscripted, it was my turn to have my hair shaved in the queue when the officer called it a day. I was rescued as usual before I could have my hair shaved the following day. The training for these conscripts was rudimentary, and they were shunted out to the war front after a couple of days of intensive training. You guessed right. A good number of these conscripts were killed.

I later joined the food directorate, and this sort of eased the hunger that I was getting used to. Till date, the last thing you will hear from me is that I am hungry.

I must confess that I took to smoking again. The only problem was that the money was not there to buy the cigarettes. I remember one incident when after buying some cigarettes, the seller unwittingly gave me my change in addition to the money I gave him. I pocketed the whole lot only to discover what happened after I got home but wouldn't be bothered correcting the mistake. I was lucky I had relatives around me who were more resourceful than I was. When you get one cigarette, this is supposed to last the whole day. You are required to put it off after a few puffs in order to reserve some for later. As always when I start, I don't stop until the cigarette is finished. Several times I found myself in situations where I resorted to begging for a puff from those who know how to save for a rainy day. These were kind relatives who knew my weakness, and they always obliged me. One of my relatives who was a banker before the war was better prepared than me. He had most of the shirts we wore for the entire duration of the war. I will never forget his kindness when things were particularly difficult for me. I had another resourceful brother who now and again bought some meat to eat with his girlfriend. He later married this lady when the war ended. They had this habit of locking me and my cousin out so that they can eat in peace. When we banged on the door persistently to raise alarm, they would be forced to let us in and share the food.

While the war lasted, education was out of the agenda. I did however undertake some private teaching sessions for friends, some of who had ulterior motives which I feigned ignorance of. While blasting away at a quadratic equation, the girl who would be expected to be paying attention would be eyeing me, pretending to be sleepy and wondering how naïve I was at not getting the message. As expected, some of those classes fell apart since I was not ready to play "hanky-panky" games.

The war was now coming to an end, and you could hear the sound of guns all around you. There was nowhere else to run to, and we now had to surrender our faith to the almighty God. We went for the usual few sticks of cigarettes, which we enjoyed, hoping that if we were going to die, a good smoke will sure do us some good. We smoked with reckless abandon, and this time around we used all the money we had on us to buy a pack of cigarettes each. The soldiers came in, and surprisingly they were friendly. We had a chat with some of them and enjoyed a drink of palm wine with them. It was as if there had been no fighting after all. The soldiers were all young boys like us, and we interacted freely with them. We made sure, however, that the girls were locked away to prevent their being "liberated" by the invading forces.

Within a few days of the war ending, we were on our way home. Home was about eighteen miles away, and I remember doing the journey with my suitcase containing few personal items mounted on my head. It was a journey we undertook with joy. The only problem was that we were not sure what home was like. The houses could have been destroyed. We were not even sure whether our parents were alive or dead. The last we heard from them was two years back.

On my way, a soldier who was manning a checkpoint ordered me to stop and open my suitcase for a search. He claimed I looked like a Biafran soldier. He ransacked my stuff and ended up taking a few things that he liked. I thanked him profusely for letting me go. He could have killed me, and nobody would have batted an eyelid. You can imagine how painful and heartrending it was to thank a soldier who had just taken some valued items from my luggage.

Getting home and finding that we had a place we could call home was a pleasure indeed. My parents survived. My siblings including my younger brother who was an officer survived and came home walking and jogging through a distance of well over fifty miles. My cousin, the one I spent some time with at the war front, also survived. I lost a young cousin, and this was a small price to pay considering that some families were wiped out.

There were stories to be exchanged as to how we survived. The most distressing problem was feeding. There was no money to buy food with. This was a major problem until relief materials started flowing in from Caritas International. One of my cousins secured employment with this organization, and he made sure the family had a good supply of food. He offered to introduce me to his boss so that I can join him with the distribution of relief materials. I declined the offer because I did not want anything that would interfere with my lifelong ambition of becoming a doctor. It took a lot of courage and determination to be able to decline a job offer that would have guaranteed food for the entire family soon after the civil war.

Life was coming back to normal, and schools were beginning to resume. I secured a job in the same institution I was working at before the war started. I was back to receiving my monthly salary as before. My parents were back to the same place they were. With my salary, I was able to buy myself some cigarettes and was now smoking openly. Having survived the war, I felt I was matured enough to do whatever I wanted. The students and some of my colleagues who were missing from school were obviously those that did not survive the war. I recommenced teaching science and mathematics. The swagger was back, and the sky was now the limit one more time.

I applied and secured admission to the medical school. Securing this admission was not without a hitch. Since postal services were at best rudimentary, I gave my application form to a friend who was travelling to the city where the university was. This gentleman for some reason did not submit my application. I remained waiting anxiously for a response from the university, and nothing was forthcoming. One day, a senior colleague told me that rather than stay waiting for a response from the university, why don't I take a trip there to find out what was going on? I did, and as God would have it, the very day I got there was the last day they were compiling the final list of the candidates that had been accepted.

My application was not submitted, and consequently my name was not in the list. It dawned on me that I was going to waste another year before reapplying. The registrar who was compiling the list knew my family and helped by accepting and going through my documents there and then. I made the cut off mark, and my name made the list. Everything happened through a thirty-minute window before he stepped out to submit the list to the dean faculty of medicine. I made it by a whisker.

There is a quote in Latin "*Vox populi est vox Dei*"—"The voice of the people is the voice of God." That senior colleague who spoke to me was God-sent. When I met this gentleman several years after, he did not have a clue what he did for me to warrant a special gift from me.

The medical school I attended was a brand new one opened by academicians from my part of Nigeria, who felt they were no longer safe going back to their former places of work before the civil war. We were the pioneer students of this institution, and the responsibility was on us to make the institution the best in Nigeria, if not Africa. The professors were world renowned academicians who were dedicated and determined to face challenges brought on by the just ended civil war. Holidays were deemed a pleasure we could not afford. Our syllabus was modeled after the British system, and examiners were brought over now and again to assess us.

Financial support was not much of a problem because the State and Federal Government were now offering scholarship to help students. There was always a bit of money left over after paying for tuition and boarding which we use as pocket money to help us get along.

The intensive and rigorous training notwithstanding. Life was a far cry from the suffering we endured while the civil war lasted. The five years went by quickly without the disruptions that are common now. Examiners came over from the United Kingdom as usual for the final examination. They expressed surprise at the level of our standard which they acknowledged was comparable with that of any medical school of repute in the United Kingdom.

I made it, and now I have achieved my lifelong ambition of becoming a doctor. I bought a brand new car for the very first time in my life, and the swagger came back.

To clip my wings before I fly away like a bird, my father summoned me one day and cautioned me. "Young man, you can never qualify as a good doctor except if you go abroad to do your post graduate training." There was no way he was going to let me continue to roam the streets playing the young doctor while I still had several years of studying ahead of me, and I had only just begun.

So far, one can see the influence of my parents in my life. Those were the days when parents had strong influence on the upbringing of their kids. In my part of the world, there was nothing like "I am now eighteen years old and therefore I can decide for myself what is good or bad for me." You say this to your parents at your own peril.

The fear of your parents was the beginning of wisdom. Bringing a girlfriend home was inconceivable. You will recall that I was summoned to answer questions just because it was suspected that I had a girlfriend. As a matter of fact, the first time a girlfriend came to see my parents was the lady I was engaged to, and marriage was very much on the cards.

As faith would have it one more time, I did my one-year internship at a hospital only a stone throw away from my parents. Here we go again, with my parents, for reasons I do not have any answer to, hanging around me. Except for going home to eat now and again, I stayed well away, confined in my residence in the hospital. The proximity however was such that my parents got to hear what mischief I was up to away from their prying eyes.

I worked hard in that hospital and the one year of internship went swiftly bye without problems.

I was now ready for the compulsory one year of national service referred to as National Youth Service Corp (NYSC). This program I gathered is still ongoing. It is designed to expose young graduates to other cultures with a view to enhancing national unity and understanding.

I was posted to a hospital and was working with an Egyptian consultant in obstetrics and gynaecology. He was the gentleman that got me interested in the field. He had the habit of abandoning me to get on with the job while he went about his private business. The director of the hospital was also an Egyptian who was not as qualified as he was and consequently could not call him to order.

On my part, however, I was a dashing young man with a flashy car to boot and a streak of stubbornness. There was an incident I will recall when we both abandoned our patients unattended. I went home and parked my car at the back of my house to avoid detection. The director of the hospital came calling and for some reason, suspecting I was home, came to the back of the house where he found my car nicely parked. The problem was that he was very short and could not gain access through my window to catch me red-handed. After several minutes of shouting my name, he left and went back to the hospital. The next day he summoned me to his office and gave me a bit of talking to. I was not bothered, and he knew he needed me in the hospital more than I did—certainly not with the pittance that went for salary.

The one year of national service was soon over, and I was back home to figure out my next line of action.

The next line of action was saving up whatever income that came my way and getting ready to travel to the United Kingdom for my postgraduate training. I had made up my mind it was obstetrics and gynecology and nothing else. With a bit of help from family and friends, I was able to save a good amount I felt should be adequate to help me survive the first few months until I was able to secure a job.

Fourth Phase (1976–1986)

Securing accommodation in the United Kingdom was difficult, and on some occasions, I had the door shut to my face because I was not the person they anticipated I was. I had problems figuring out why I was being rejected despite the fact that my voice for starters gave me away as a male and probably from Africa. Luckily, a family was glad to let me into a spare bedroom, and I remained there quietly like the good boy that I was. I had to jealously guard against frivolous spending. Going to the shop to buy a drink or to the pub for a pint of beer was out of the question. I was determined not to run out of money until I secured a job. Some doctors that came over with me at the same time had to flee back to Nigeria because they could not cope with the hardship.

Unfortunately for me, I arrived the United Kingdom during winter. For someone who had never seen snow before, the ordeal of getting used to the cold that came with it was unimaginable. The problem was compounded by the fact that the snow that year was considered the worst for several years. This was the main reason some other colleagues could not continue. I had to hang in there because I had no choice. My father for starters would not tolerate me coming back without achieving what I set out for. I survived the winter and settled in to get on with my studies. On reflection, it would have been better to arrive during summer to be able to gradually adapt to the cold weather that we were not used to in Africa.

At school, we were taught that something was "as white as snow" without a clue what snow was all about. I learnt the hard way the dos and don'ts of life under snowy condition. This included abandoning my immaculate white suit and a white shoe to match that I travelled to the United Kingdom with. The embarrassment was such that I refused to wear it even during summer just in case. The first day I ventured out appearing dapper in my white suit and matching shoes, I noticed that people were staring at me in a way I could not understand. It was when I got home that my friend sympathetically informed me that it was my outfit that was the cause. The experience was very embarrassing indeed.

I passed all the examinations I sat for that year, and I was good to go for a job in a hospital. I secured a job easily and was now focused on getting on with my ambition of becoming a specialist in obstetrics and gynecology.

Working in a foreign land for the very first time was not without its ups and downs. I had earlier recounted my escapades as a young trainee doctor and would not be repeating them here.

Whether you are that way disposed or not, I realized that you must always pretend to be happy and courteous to everybody. On some occasions, one forgets to add "please "or "thank you" in whatever sentence one makes. I remember one occasion when I was operating in theatre, and my assisting nurse refused to hand me an instrument simply because I did not add please. You learn the hard way, don't you?

No matter how tired you are as a junior doctor, you are required to have a permanent smile on your face, even if you are at the point of dropping dead. It takes time to get used to all the shenanigans, and this is more so for a doctor coming from a country where you get away, albeit unwittingly, with what could be construed as rudeness in other places. Talk about culture shock. Britain has a way of brushing you up to be very polite and courteous no matter the circumstances you find yourself in. You forget to add "please" to every sentence you make at your peril.

To get on with my colleagues and other members of staff, I hid that stubborn streak about me and remained a very good and well-liked doctor. This bit of me came up, however, when it suddenly dawned on me that for some reason people were not calling me by my surname—a surname that was by all intents and purposes very easy to pronounce was deemed difficult, and I was made to spell it always.

To make matters worse, other colleagues with what could pass as very difficult names did not have problems, obviously because they came from the "right" places. This was one of the reasons I refused to change or modify my accent, and I made sure everybody got the pronunciation and spelling of my surname right. "I am not good at foreign names" was a constant refrain by colleagues. These same individuals will pronounce and spell to the letter, some mundane names without vowels from Eastern Europe.

As a trainee junior doctor or an intern, if you like, you were not limited to one hospital, and you are required to transfer to another hospital after six months. You might, if you are particularly lucky, get one year before moving on. This is one of the reasons you have to be in your best behavior as you will need a reference from your consultant for job interviews. You have to smile all the time and clown now and again for members of staff to be in his good books. You learn to pretend that all is well even when you consider him a downright racist or SOB.

You have to attend several interviews before you get an offer. In some situations, there is already a local chap they have reserved the job for, but because the law requires that there has to be an interview, they get candidates from all over the place. The candidates get paid transportation fee.

When you get called back in after all the candidates have been interviewed, you have been offered the job. The rest of the candidates will now start getting ready to hit the road.

It was with this mindset that I applied for a job in a big teaching hospital, fully convinced there was no way I was going to be accepted. This was one occasion where I was very relaxed as I was in no illusion I was going to be accepted.

When I was called into the interview room, I was not intimidated by the eminent professors that sat across the other side of the table facing me. There was a story making the round in those days that once the interviewers start asking questions unrelated to the program, you might as well consider yourself as someone who had been asked over to make up the number as the law requires.

I sat down quite relaxed with a sheepish grin all over my face. The first question I got asked was my name. One of the professors said, "Young man, now let's discuss a bit about religion." He asked whether I can tell him who the mother of Benjamin was in the Bible. He felt I should know since this was my first name. Here was someone training to be an obstetrician and gynaecologist being asked a biblical question during an interview. In this type of situation, no matter how determined you are, nervousness always gets at you. I forgot the name.

When he reminded me that it was Rachael, I said, "There you are." I knew it was Rachael, but the name just escaped my memory. Boldly, since it was now obvious the job was not for me, I told the professor that I was now going to give a brief lecture about Rachael and the reason I was determined to be an obstetrician. They all burst out laughing at my audacity and boldness. They sat back and allowed me to go on with my lecture. I informed them that it was because Racheal died while giving birth to Benjamin, I was determined to make it up for Rachael. This was what informed my desire to become an obstetrician. All that I was asking for is to be accepted in a good teaching hospital to enable me to fulfill my ambition.

They enjoyed my story and my boldness, and that was the end of the interview. When I left the room, I started getting ready to hit the road, and I was in no mood to wait until the end of the interview. I had to wait however in order to leave my details for the travel allowance.

After all the candidates had been interviewed, to my greatest surprise, I was called back in, and I was offered the job. They obviously bought my story about Rachael. To cut a long story short, not only was I accepted in the hospital, I also went through a very intensive training program. I was kept in the hospital until I finished my internship and passed my professional examination. As a Christian, it is my belief that Rachael also had a hand in all that happened to me. Fast forward several years after my training. I have been actively involved with the improvement of maternal mortality in sub-Saharan Africa without realizing that this was a pledge I made during my formative years as an obstetrician.

I will now delve into how I ended up in Saudi Arabia. As a young obstetrician from a third-world country, there was at that time enormous pressure to get you back home to help. Such was the demand that I succumbed to pressure and agreed to attend a job interview in Nigeria. I kept an open mind, and I was determined to relocate if the offer was good.

This was what happened at the interview. I was the sole candidate. The interview panel was made up of about twelve individuals. The chairman was a colleague and a friend I knew specialized in public health. I gathered there was no obstetrician or gynaecologist in the panel. After I made myself comfortable in my allotted seat, the next thing I heard was "What are the causes of ectopic pregnancy?"

I was taken aback because this was not expected. Without giving the question a thought, I said, "Hold it right there, gentlemen. Is this supposed to be an academic exercise or what?" I cracked a joke that got them laughing. I informed them that if I knew I was coming for an academic exercise, I would have done a bit of reading to prepare. I just couldn't believe it.

Here was a doctor who had gone through his training and worked at a senior level in the United Kingdom being made to answer questions I would under normal circumstances ask a medical student on rotation in the field. I answered the question, and at the end of the interview after I had been offered the job, I was requested to make available to the ministry of health all my previous academic certificates. I was reminded to include my elementary school certificate and the rest. When I asked what my elementary school certificate had to do with my job as a gynaecologist and obstetrician, I was told that they are required to look at the totality of my education to help them make an informed decision about my intelligence. I was also required to buy a folder with all the certificates enclosed. I agreed, thanked them profusely, and left.

I did not accept the job and did not make any effort to inform them that I was no longer interested in the job. I boarded the plane after one-week en route to the United Kingdom and thereafter made no further attempt to secure a job in Nigeria or any other African country.

I came back to Britain to continue my job as a middle grade obstetrician and gynaecologist. It was during this period that I was introduced to a gentleman who claimed to be a pilot from the United States on vacation. He claimed to have spent a couple of weeks in Nigeria and visited a number of places of interest. The fact that he had some interesting stories to tell about his escapades in Nigeria endeared him to me. When I told him about my plans to visit Belgium to buy a left-hand drive car that I intended to ship to Nigeria, he quickly volunteered to help as he knew the places to go for good deals on brand-new Mercedes Benz cars. I trusted him and, without giving the idea a thought, parted with my hard-earned savings for the deal. As soon as he got hold of my cash, he disappeared into thin air and was never to be seen again. I kept waiting for my car to no avail.

Fifth Phase (1986–1996)

It was in this condition of anxiety and depression that a colleague of mine from Saudi Arabia talked me into considering working in Saudi Arabia where I will be in a position to quickly save the amount that was stolen to buy me a new car. Prior to this, I had never entertained the idea of visiting any country in the Middle East, not to talk of picking a job there. What my Saudi colleague did was to write to the Saudi Embassy without my consent to invite me for an interview. I was surprised to receive an invitation for an interview for a job I never applied for from the Saudi Arabian Embassy in London.

I went for the interview, and I was promptly offered a job with the ministry of health as a specialist. The salary, when compared with what I was currently receiving in the United Kingdom, could only be described as "mouth-watering." I quickly succumbed to the temptation and packed up ready for yet another adventure. My Saudi colleague reassured me that I will not regret my decision to relocate. He also said that as soon as he was through with his training, he will be back home and hopefully will meet me there. He laughed when I mentioned that I was panicky over the stringent laws that Saudi Arabia was known for. All he said was that if I remained the gentleman that he knows I am, I would not have any reason to fear.

I went to Saudi Arabia as planned, and I must confess that the stringent laws I was panicking about were simply ways of normal life that were quite easy to adapt to. Alcoholics have everything to be afraid of, and if you are one, Saudi Arabia is not a place for you. Why bother when you can have your fill during your vacation away from the kingdom? I needed time, however, to get through the initial culture shock.

I found the Saudis very friendly and welcoming to foreigners. The fabled and well-acknowledged Arabian hospitality is very much on display in Saudi Arabia. When you get invited over for a meal, it is always a sumptuous meal, the type you have never seen before. Your Saudi host derives much pleasure and pride when you are very well satisfied with his hospitality. You are not required to belch as a sign of satisfaction we were made to believe.

I will spend some time to describe a typical Saudi meal. It is usually a well-spiced and cooked rice served in a big basin or tray and a whole barbequed or roasted sheep, depending on the number of guests, placed on top. Guests sit on a mat, and you get to use your hand to deal with the food.

Assorted fruits adorn the entire service mat, and you help your-self to whatever tickles your fancy.

After you have had your fill, you top up the meal with a scented and aromatic tea or coffee. While the meal is ongoing, your host will suffuse your body with the aroma of frankincense or other scents that are found only in that part of the world. But I can attest to the fact that many a time you leave with a protruding tummy from a good meal.

Those of us that were single looked forward to the invite which occurred very frequently, and on some occasions, we leave with a good sampling of food wrapped up for use at other times. As my colleague in the United Kingdom predicted, I enjoyed every bit of my stay, and I quickly adapted and got on with my job.

Saudi hospitality extends to the women also. A colleague's wife told a story of what happened when she was invited to a party by her friend. Her friend admonished her that she must appear in her best attire since she was going to introduce her to the rest of her companions.

The doctor's wife made sure she appeared in her "Sunday best" so as not to disappoint her friend. When she got there, her friend pulled her aside and told her that under no circumstance was she going to introduce her because she was deemed not to be wearing what was considered acceptable.

The lady took her to a room, opened her wardrobe filled with assorted designer attires, and asked her to select one and change to it. She did, and her friend was impressed. After the party, the lady made sure she left with a good sampling of designer wear just in case another party comes calling. This is Saudi hospitality for you. What my colleague's wife considered her best and most expensive wear was considered a trash by her Saudi friend.

After a year with the ministry of health, I was promoted to the post of consultant in obstetrics and gynaecology and later to the position of head of the department. It was while I was in this position that the Saudi Arabian oil company got to know me and offered me a job with the company. I enjoyed my stay in Saudi Arabia to the extent that I was ready to continue working and probably retire thereafter. It was while I was working with the ministry of health that I got to know about the oil company—a company that offered better prospects and remuneration than the health ministry. Naturally I focused my attention towards securing a job there, and I succeeded. I had to relocate to the United Kingdom for about one year before commencing the oil company job.

Sixth Phase (1996–2006)

It was while I was working with the oil company that I travelled to Istanbul in Turkey to recuperate after a bout of chest infection brought on by excessive smoking. I gave up smoking after this infection and have remained a nonsmoker ever since.

With members of my family now on tow, we spent many vacations in Dubai as well as the United Kingdom. Looking for a new location for our vacation, we chose Phuket in Thailand, only to abandon it for some inexplicable reason in favour of Dubai once again. The reason became apparent when the first ever earthquake followed by a devastating tsunami occurred in the region. The resort village in Phuket was destroyed, and many tourists lost their lives. This incident happened three weeks after we were scheduled to be there. This could very well pass as a narrow escape once again. I daresay I never dreamt of going to Thailand ever again.

My job with the Saudi Arabian oil company was a lot more challenging, but I did enjoy every bit of my stay with the company. The job came with all sorts of fringe benefits including first or business-class air travels. Also you are allowed to travel to the United States and other countries for academic meetings or symposia once a year with all expenses paid.

It was during one of these trips that I met my Saudi colleague who recommended the Middle East job for me, way back in the United Kingdom. He was now the dean of the faculty of medicine in one of the medical schools in Saudi Arabia. He was glad to see me and was happy to hear that I was enjoying my job in his country as he predicted. He promised he would come over in the evening to my hotel to pick me up for a sightseeing tour of Jeddah.

At the conference, there was this massive Mercedes Benz car with gold-plated logos parked around the corner. I concluded this must belong to the prince that came over to open the conference. When in the evening, my colleague pulled over to pick me up with the same car I saw at the conference premises earlier, I could not believe my eyes. I told him I saw the car and concluded it must belong to a prince. He smiled and asked me to hop in. One of the places he took me to was the Red Sea and other important landmarks in Jeddah, Saudi Arabia.

Working with the Saudi Arabian oil company, an American-managed health organization, enabled me to secure a USA permanent green card for the entire family. My family left for the United States two years before the expiration of my ten-year contract.

Working with the Saudi Arabian oil company was not all about exotic holidays and living life to the full. It was during this period that I went with my family to Nigeria and opened a health care centre in a remote area that we felt needed some form of health care service, albeit for screening purposes only. A nurse practitioner was employed to run the facility, and the unit was left under the management of the Catholic parish priest in the area. The nurse was admonished that under no circumstances should anybody be turned away based on religion or whatever.

The unit was designed to provide basic healthcare screening procedure and dispensing of over the counter medications (OTC) including multivitamins and folic acid to pregnant women. The overall aim, however, was to identify patients that hitherto would not have gone to the hospital for proper medical checkup and treatment. It was a fulfilling venture, and the degree of appreciation shown by the community was heartwarming indeed.

Prior to my final departure from Saudi Arabia, I had a series of send-off parties and presents from the company, friends, and colleagues for creditable performance and dedication to duty throughout the period I was in Saudi Arabia. To crown it all, I did not at any time fall foul of the law, and I left the kingdom with all my body parts intact.

This goes to prove that the law in Saudi Arabia is nothing to be afraid of, and I can say without fear of contradiction that the period

I spent in the kingdom remained the best during my entire career as an obstetrician and gynaecologist.

I considered this period the pinnacle of my practice, and it was my intention thereafter to gradually wind down towards retirement.

Obstetrics practice is the most demanding of all the other branches of medicine. It is also the branch that is likely to get you into trouble should anything go wrong. Over the years, we are made to believe that, should you retire at an age pretty much to the right of sixty-five years of age, chances are that you probably would be left with only two years to live before death comes calling. Working as an obstetrician in a busy hospital in the western world drains so much life out of you that over a long period of time takes its toll.

It might be pertinent to add at this juncture that while I had the financial support to meet all my commitments including annual dues for the awards, I had the following accolades to my name:

Fellow of the Society of Obstetricians
& Gynaecologists of Canada

Fellow of the International College of Surgeons

Associate Fellow of the American College
of Obstetricians & Gynaecologists

Fellow of the Royal College of Obstetricians
& Gynaecologists (London)

I was a reviewer of journals for McMaster University Department of Health Sciences, Hamilton, Ontario, Canada for evidence-based clinical practice.

I was the author of several publications in reputable international journals while I was in the United Kingdom and Saudi Arabia.

I have a book entitled *Pregnancy: A continuing source of sorrow and pain for women in sub-Saharan Africa.*

You will recall my pledge to my interviewers several years back to avenge the death of the biblical Rachael during childbirth.

Surprisingly, over the years I have had a passion over the issue of high maternal mortality in third-world countries, especially in sub-Saharan Africa. I did not recall the pledge I made several years ago in jest having anything to do with my interest.

This is one aspect of my life that is fascinating, and I am glad I am able to connect the dots through my power of recollection.

I have highlighted my qualification above with a sense of fulfillment and humility and not in a boastful manner. This is just to indicate that through all the obstacles and adversities I finally arrived at my destiny.

Seventh Phase (2006–2016)

Now back in the United States to join the family, I decided to stay off jobs to enable me to spend quality time with my family. This was not to last for a long period of time as anticipated. I felt bored and overwhelmed with the desire to get back to work.

Going back to clinical practice was not on the cards because of the high level of litigations among obstetricians and gynaecologist in the United States. This bit of information was gathered from colleagues from the United States employed by the company. Also having not had prior working experience in the United States, I considered it a recipe for disaster going into clinical practice. I spent ten months working as a volunteer lecturer with a medical faculty before a job came beckoning from the United Kingdom.

Since a nonclinical appointment was not forthcoming in the United States, I decided to accept the offer from the United Kingdom.

Because the family was unwilling to relocate, I was faced with a decision dilemma—accept to work in the United Kingdom on part-time basis to enable me to come back home regularly for the sake of the kids or abandon the offer and continue looking for a job in the United States. I chose the former and made it a point of duty to come home for three weeks' vacation after every three months on the job.

This decade was unremarkable because it involved travelling to and fro the United States and the United Kingdom across the Atlantic.

There was a difference between the travels this period and previous travels while I was working with the Saudi Arabian oil company. I got used to flying economy class and going for the cheapest ticket that was available. The money was no longer free-flowing, and I had to be prudent with my expenditures. I did not mind being the last to board a flight and sitting at the tail end of the flight most of the times.

My guiding principle in life is that when the going is good, you enjoy it, and while you are at it, you should not forget or look down on those that are less privileged. When things turn around, as nothing lasts forever, you should also enjoy it and never ever envy those that are more privileged than you. With humility as your guiding principle, you should be able to adapt to any situation you find yourself.

It was during this decade that my father died, followed by my mom within a space of two months. We all knew there was no way my mother was going to carry on without her husband. They had been inseparable all their lives. We cracked a joke telling her to make sure she does not follow her husband without giving us some time to recover. She smiled and said nothing. She had her plans which she was not ready to divulge. She died quietly within two months after my father, and we found ourselves back to planning another funeral yet again.

They both lived a very fulfilled life. He died at the age of a hundred and six, and my mother at the age of eighty-six years. My mother used to be referred to as a human alarm clock because of her lifelong habit of waking up at six every morning throughout her adult life to go to the church for morning devotion.

My job in the United Kingdom involved travelling around. I spent time in Scotland, Wales, and England but did not have the opportunity to visit Northern Ireland and Ireland.

I will round up this decade by mentioning that this was the period I decided to call it a day and retire from clinical practice. As is usual with my life, the hospital where I started my practice in the United Kingdom was the same hospital I worked at before retiring. This was after several years of service including traveling to the Middle East and uncountable number of hospitals in the United Kingdom. It was certainly more than can pass as a mere coincidence. I left the United Kingdom in 2016 back to the United States for my retirement.

Since this decade marks the end of my life as an obstetrician and gynaecologist, I will mention some of the remarkable events that occurred during my practice. I will mention briefly some observations and experience I acquired through my practice in the various continents I worked in.

In the area of maternal mortality, which is an area I found myself drawn to as discussed previously, I encountered four maternal deaths I was involved with, albeit indirectly, during my almost four decades of intense clinical practice.

The first was during my second year as a budding obstetrician in Nigeria during the compulsory National Youth Corp programme. This was a maternal death that occurred due to anaesthetic complication. This was before the caesarean operation that I was going to perform had even started. While I was scrubbing for the operation, the nurse informed me that there was a problem and that the patient had died. Being a young and inexperienced doctor, I abandoned what I was doing and rushed to the phone to get hold of the consultant on duty with me. He did not show up, but he advised that I should try to get the baby out. By the time I got back to the patient, the baby also died, and the operation was abandoned. To the best of my knowledge, nothing came of this matter.

The second maternal death occurred in Saudi Arabia due to excessive bleeding during instrumental delivery by a registrar. The registrar tried to get hold of the consultant who was on duty with him but could not get hold of him. Unable to get hold of the consultant, I was summoned, and despite not being on-call I rushed over. Unfortunately by the time I got there, the patient was dead from excessive bleeding.

The other maternal death was in the United Kingdom. Maternal death was due to complications of severe pre-eclampsia. I was involved because I delivered the patient through caesarean section and was actively involved with the management of her intra-partum pre-eclampsia.

The other maternal death I heard about but was not involved with the management occurred in Saudi Arabia. Maternal death occurred as a result of sickle cell crisis during labour.

While I would have wished that no maternal deaths occurred during my watch, these are unavoidable events for any actively practicing obstetrician. At the end of the day, the joy of any obstetrician is when your patients, mother and child, are brought safely to the world without problems.

In terms of experience acquired during my practice and travels, I will briefly mention a few since this discussion is not about my clinical practice.

After treating several cases of vesico-vaginal fistula (VVF) and recto-vaginal fistula (RVF) during my year of national service in Nigeria, I did not come across any similar case throughout several decades of practice in Europe and Saudi Arabia.

Compared with women in Africa and Europe, Saudi women have what can be described as the best obstetric performance in whatever category. No matter the number of women coming to the hospital in labour, they all tend to deliver with minimal interference from doctors and midwives. Before you know it, they are back home to commence limbering up for a repeat performance.

In Europe, all you need is four to five women in labour at any given moment, and you are sure of having a sleepless night managing all sorts of complication.

My observation about Saudi women was confirmed by a group of obstetricians who published recently that the reason Saudi women have a very good obstetric performance is due to the consumption of dates during pregnancy and labour.

If I knew about this earlier, I would have published my observation long before they did. One thing I knew for certain was that Saudi women pray to God to grant them the same rapid and excellent delivery as Mary did during her birth of Jesus. Many Christians do not know about this. The other observation is that sickle cell disease does not have any significant effect on pregnant women in Saudi Arabia. They go through pregnancy and have their babies with little or no effect whatsoever. Compared with women from Africa, a good percentage of women die from complications of sickle cell disease during childhood. Pregnancy and labour are usually turbulent and in some cases could lead to death. The reason for this is because sicklers in Saudi Arabia have a large percentage of fetal haemoglobin with large oxygen carrying capacity, the reverse is the case for women with similar condition in sub-Saharan Africa.

These are my observation worth mentioning. In conclusion, however, I remain grateful to my spiritual mother Rachael for being there for me during all those years of very intensive clinical practice as an obstetrician and gynaecologist. You will recall my pledge during the interview for a job several year back. I can confirm that I never for one moment remember this pledge throughout my several years of practice—until the very moment I decided to write this story.

Eight Phase (2016–Till Date)

I am now a senior citizen. Waking up late in the mornings and watching things happen around me. I have weaned myself from the hospital bleep that controls your life when on normal duty and on-call. The bleep that typically goes off summoning for an emergency after you have tucked yourself in bed and just about to go to sleep after a busy night on call. When that bleep goes off, whatever you are doing must be abandoned to go attend to an emergency. This is what obstetrics practice is all about.

I do now and again have the urge to go back to practice, but with age not being on my side, this remains only a wishful thinking.

My passion for maternal health remains undimished though. I undertake lectures here in the United States and Africa on topics related to maternal health.

My father, as I stated earlier, died at the age of 106. I am silently praying that I should be able to add a few more decades to my life span. I hope this is not a wishful thinking as God has his plans for each and every one of us.

I will summarize by highlighting those aspects of my life I mentioned in this story that could be construed as a miracle or unexplained phenomenon.

- The apparition or vision of a fair mother and child when I was just about three to four years old and tugging at my mother's feet, seeking attention.
- The marking of the cross on my forehead with a chalk or any marker—a reflex action that could not be explained, and every attempt to stop the habit failed.

- The old lady that mysteriously appeared at midnight to stop my father and I embarking on what was a perilous journey to the hospital.
- The near drowning of my mother in a deep pond with me at the age of six standing there watching helplessly.
- The promotion and transfer of my father from a remote village to a city that was only one mile away from my high school. He expressed a wish when he took me for the interview, and his wish came through.
- The snake that slithered in to bite a young houseboy who opened the door to let us in late at night while we both escaped unharmed.
- The prophecy by a palmist that predicted at the height of the civil war that I would travel the world—a period I was not sure of surviving a ferocious civil war in Nigeria.
- Making attempts against the wishes of my parents to join the army during the civil war but was rebuffed and ordered to go back home. My friends who were less qualified were accepted, and a good number of them perished.
- Traveling without informing my parents a couple of days before a bomb was dropped right at the top of the house where we relax as young teenagers, with nothing to do during the civil war. Many of my friends perished in the bombing.
- Finally it is worth mentioning that I was the only young lad in my group who was not able to shoot and kill a bird with my catapult. Despite the ridicule, I just did not succeed.
- Making the cut into acceptance into the medical school at the end of the civil was with only thirty minutes to spare. Failure would have meant missing a whole year before reapplying.

In conclusion, I quote from the Songs of Solomon as written in Proverbs 1:8–9:

> My son, hear the instructions of thy father
> and forsake not the law of thy mother; for they

shall be an ornament of Grace unto thy head and
chains about thy neck.

This quote from Proverbs applies to my relationship with my parents as this story highlights. My life was intertwined with my parents well into adulthood. They were there for me at all times. Though I did not realize it at the time, their love for me was unquestionable. Being close by wherever I went during my formative years was not intentional but through what can aptly be referred to as divine intervention.

Their love for every member of the family was the same, and no one of us had any iota of special privilege or love. I succeeded simply because of the love and respect I had for them. I listened to their advice and at no time did I consider them unworthy of admonishing or advising me.

When at the age of 102, my father fell and broke his femur, he felt that the time was up and that there was no need fighting to stay alive. He summoned all of us for an urgent meeting. He stressed during this meeting that nothing will make him happier than we remain at peace with one another at all times. He spoke as if he was going to leave us for good.

I was frightened, more so because I had always suspected that because of his faith, he could go to bed and just die without fanfare.

At the end of the meeting after everyone had gone, I went back to my father and demanded a one-to-one meeting with him. I asked him what his intention was in summoning us for the meeting. I said to him without mincing words that if it was his intention to die, he should forget the idea as we were quite capable of taking care of him for many more years to come. I just wanted to reassure him he was not a burden to us. I took him by surprise. He was speechless, looked at me for a while, and thanked me. As God would have it, my father recovered from his fall and had four more years added to his life.

If parents take more interest in the affairs of their children, and children show more respect to their parents, the world would be a better pace for everybody.

Respect for parents will also help us when we derail in our pursuit of our destiny to trace our way back. It is like finding your way out while meandering through the maze of life.

I will end by quoting the only one of the Ten Commandments that comes with a reward or promise as found in Exodus 20:12 which states as follows:

"Honour thy father and thy mother that thy days may be long upon the land which the Lord thy God giveth thee."

This is my story.

About the Author

T he author is a naturalized United States citizen, an African immi-grant, originally from Nigeria.

He has four children and three grandchildren, all at various stages of their academic pursuit.

The early stage of the author's life, as depicted in this book, was in the '50s in Nigeria. It is remarkable that the author was able to remember and recount events that occurred in his life, even at the tender age of three.

He was educated in Nigeria until he obtained his degree in med-icine from the University of Nigeria in 1975. After completing the one-year horsemanship and the compulsory one-year national ser-vice programmes, he proceeded to the United Kingdom for special-ization in obstetrics and gynaecology. He completed this programme in 1983 and was subsequently admitted as a fellow in the specialty by the Royal College of Obstetricians and Gynaecologists in London United Kingdom (FRCOG).

His experience in his field of specialization was acquired from three continents where he practiced—Africa, Europe, and Asia.

He is the author of several publications in reputable interna-tional journals in obstetrics and gynaecology.

His interest in maternal health led to the publication of his book titled *Pregnancy: A continuing source of sorrow and pain for women in sub-Saharan Africa.*

He has also written articles aimed at women's health in Nigeria. Two recent feature articles in Nigeria-world website come to mind: "The Demystification of Uterine Fibroid" and "Female Genital Cancer—Prevention Better Than Cure."

Currently, he undertakes lecture schedule in the United States and Nigeria on maternal health with emphasis on maternal mortality during childbirth.

www.ingramcontent.com/pod-product-compliance
Lightning Source LLC
Chambersburg PA
CBHW051647120626
46551CB00015B/2258